Travel Guide To Funchal 2024

Discover the Hidden Gems of Funchal

Jason J. Jones

Copyright © 2023 Jason J. Jones

All rights reserved. No part of this publication may be reproduced, distributed, or transmitted in any form or by any means, including photocopying, recording, or other electronic or mechanical methods, without the prior written permission of the publisher.

Table Of Contents

INTRODUCTION
Welcome to Funchal

GETTING READY FOR YOUR FUNCHAL ADVENTURE
Planning Your Trip

Packing Essentials

Language and Currency

ARRIVING IN FUNCHAL
Funchal Airport and Transportation

Navigating the City

EXPLORING THE CITY
The Heart of Funchal

Historical and Cultural Sites

Local Cuisine and Dining

OUTDOOR ADVENTURES

HIDDEN GEMS AND LOCAL SECRETS
Off the Beaten Path Attractions
Funchal's Best-Kept Secrets
Meeting the Locals

DAY TRIPS AND EXCURSIONS
Exploring Beyond Funchal
Island Hopping Adventures
Tips for Organizing Day Trips

PRACTICAL INFORMATION
Accommodation Options
Health and Safety Tips
Useful Phrases and Etiquette

FUNCHAL IN 2024: EVENTS AND FESTIVALS
Noteworthy Events and Festivals

Planning Your Visit Around Special Occasions

APPENDICES

Sample Itineraries

Useful Contacts and Information

INTRODUCTION

Welcome to Funchal

Situated on the lovely island of Madeira, Funchal is a quaint and energetic city that entices visitors with its distinct fusion of historical sites, natural beauty, and local culture. You'll have an amazing experience as soon as you get off the plane and enter the centre of this breathtaking location.

1. The capital of Madeira, Funchal, is a city of contradictions. It skillfully blends a rich historical past with a contemporary, energetic ambiance.

   The Atlantic Ocean, which envelops the island, will welcome you with open arms the moment you arrive. The rough rocks and deep blue waters make for a striking background for your voyage.

2. An important feature of the city is its historic district, or "Zona Velha." When you stroll along its winding cobblestone lanes, you'll come across modest cafes, stores owned by artists, and vibrant buildings decorated with blossoming flowers.

   These historic lanes are a delightful site to explore, bringing Funchal's past to life.

3. Moreover, Funchal is renowned for its thriving marketplaces, like the Mercado dos Lavradores. A veritable rainbow of locally made products, exotic flowers, and fresh produce can be found here.

   These marketplaces' aromas, hues, and vibrant activity are experiences in and of themselves. Remember to sample some of the region's well-known

Madeira wine and customary dishes like "espetada" or "black scabbardfish" at dining establishments.

4. Funchal is the starting point for verdant landscapes for those who love the outdoors. The outstanding array of plant species at Funchal's Botanical Garden provides a serene environment for a stroll.

Take a stroll along the island's Levada paths if you're feeling daring. These winding irrigation channels offer unmatched vistas of Madeira's breathtaking landscape as they wind through forests, beside waterfalls, and along cliff faces.

5. Art and culture enthusiasts are also catered to in Funchal. The city is home to galleries and museums that preserve Madeira's past and display the

creations of regional artists. Notable cultural sites that provide an insight into the island's rich past are the Cristiano Ronaldo Museum and the Museu de Arte Sacra.

6. Funchal displays its charming side as the day gives way to night. The city's restaurants serve a variety of traditional and foreign cuisines, and the soothing glow of the streetlights brings the city to life.

The exciting nightlife, complete with live music and dancing, gives your trip an extra special touch.

Welcome to Funchal, a place where there is something new to discover, do, and enjoy around every corner. Every traveller can find something special in this charming gem of Madeira, whether they are looking for adventure, relaxation, or cultural enrichment. The friendliness, charm, and warmth of Funchal will stay with you forever, turning your trip into a treasured experience.

GETTING READY FOR YOUR FUNCHAL ADVENTURE

Planning Your Trip

The first step in making sure your vacation to Funchal, Madeira, goes smoothly and pleasurably is to plan your trip. When getting ready for your trip, keep these things in mind:

1. **Dates of Travel:**

- Select a time to visit Funchal. Take into account the weather, nearby activities, and your schedule. Although Madeira's temperature is pleasant all year round, costs and activities may change with the seasons.

2. **Transportation and Lodging:**
- Plan and reserve your travel to Funchal Airport (FNC). Additionally, decide on

appropriate lodging—a hotel, resort, or vacation rental—based on your tastes. To guarantee a comfortable stay, make sure to read reviews and ratings.

3. **Currency and Budget:**

- Establish your travel budget, taking into account costs for lodging, meals, entertainment, and mementos. Learn about the Euro, and the local currency, and think about exchanging some money before you go.

4. **Documents for Travel:**

- Make sure your passport is valid for at least six months and that it is current. You may require a visa to enter Madeira, depending on your nationality, so be sure to review the entry requirements and apply ahead of time if needed.

5. Insurance for Travel:

- It is advisable to get travel insurance that provides coverage for unanticipated incidents, medical crises, and trip cancellations. It serves as a crucial safety net in case anything unforeseen occurs.

6. Clothes and Packing:

- Based on the season and the things you want to do, make a packing list. Funchal has a temperate climate, so pack light clothing, sunscreen, a hat, and comfortable shoes.

7. Spoken Word and Verbal Exchange:

- Although English is widely used in Funchal, particularly in the tourist districts, Portuguese is the official language. It can be useful to know a few simple Portuguese phrases for conversation.

8. **Schedule and Events:**

- Do some research on the Funchal attractions and things you want to do. To get the most out of your trip, plan a flexible schedule that allows for relaxation and spontaneity.

9. **Getting Ready for Health:**

- Before your trip to Madeira, find out if you require any vaccinations. Make sure you have travel insurance that covers medical emergencies and have any required drugs.

10. **Transportation:**

- Organise your route around Madeira and Funchal. Using public transportation, hiring a car, or depending on ridesharing and taxis are some options.

11. **Travel Adapters:**

- Funchal's electrical outlets are Type C and Type F Euro Plug plugs. Don't forget to bring the right travel adaptor for your electronics.

12. **Research and Information: -**

- Learn about the main sights, regional traditions, and food options in Funchal. With this information, you'll be able to maximise your trip.

You can reduce any potential stress and enhance your enjoyment during your visit to this fascinating destination by properly organising your trip to Funchal. Remember to have an open mind and appreciate the charm that Funchal and Madeira have to offer.

Packing Essentials

It's important to take into account the local weather, the activities you have scheduled, and the length of your stay while packing for your trip to Funchal, Madeira. The following is a list of things you should pack to make sure you're ready for your trip:

1. **Apparel:**

- For the warm, temperate weather, wear lightweight, breathable apparel.
- cosy walking shoes for discovering the trails and cities.
- A lightweight jacket or pullover for chilly nights.
- Beachwear and swimsuits if you intend to visit the coast.
- For unexpected downpours, carry a small umbrella or a raincoat.

- To defend against the sun, wear a wide-brimmed hat, sunglasses, and sunscreen.

2. **Camp Equipment:**

- If you intend to hike the Levadas or partake in other outdoor activities, you should think about bringing a daypack, moisture-wicking clothes, and hiking boots.

3. **Plug-in power adapters:**

- European-style plug adapters for charging electronics.

4. Documents for Travel:

- Passport and a photocopy of important travel documents.
- Details on travel insurance.
- any required visas.

5. **Vital Signs of Health:**

- drugs with a prescription.
- A basic first aid pack should include bandages, painkillers, and disinfectant wipes, among other necessities.

6. **Travel Add-ons:**

- Travel-size hygiene products (toothpaste, soap, shampoo, etc.).
- reusable bottle of water.
- maps or travel guidebooks.
- A travel wallet or pouch to safely store vital documents.
- Laundry detergent in travel size for extended travels.

7. **Payment and Currency:**

- Enough cash in euros to cover minor expenses.
- For larger purchases, use credit/debit cards and a currency conversion app.

8. **Technology:**

- chargers for a laptop, tablet, or smartphone.

- On-the-go device recharging with a portable power bank.

- camera and mementos to record moments in time.

9. **Amusement:**

- For leisure time, read books, e-books, or find other entertainment.

10. **Language Support:** -

- A portable translation book or an app can be useful if you don't speak Portuguese well.

11. **Other:** -

- Locks for your luggage to protect your possessions.

- If you intend to spend time in nature, bring travel-sized insect repellant.

- An eye mask and travel cushion for cosy sleeping on planes.

Keep in mind that Funchal has a laid-back vibe, so you can bring only essentials with you. To ensure that your wardrobe selections are appropriate for the weather on the dates of your trip, check the forecast. Additionally, don't forget to include extra space for any mementos you may want to buy.

Language and Currency

It is essential to comprehend the local language and currency to have a seamless and pleasurable trip to Funchal, Madeira.

Speech:

1. Portuguese is the official language of Madeira, which includes Funchal. Although Portuguese is the official language, English is spoken by many, particularly in the travel and tourism sector.

    In hotels and restaurants, especially while interacting with travellers, English is often spoken. At tourist destinations, Portuguese and English are the primary languages used for signage and information.

2. Acquiring a few simple Portuguese words will improve your trip and demonstrate your appreciation for the culture. Make a good first impression by using phrases like "Olá" (hello), "Obrigado/a" (thank you), and "Por favour" (please).

Money:

1. The Euro (€) is the currency that is used in Funchal and all of Madeira. Several European nations use the same currency.

   It is advised to carry some cash in euros for little purchases and locations that might not take credit or debit cards. ATMs in Funchal allow you to take out euros using a debit or credit card.

In most hotels, restaurants, and retail establishments in Funchal, credit and debit cards are accepted. It is advisable to notify your bank of your trip arrangements to avoid any problems when using your card overseas.

Additionally, for convenience, think about carrying a modest amount of local cash, particularly in less visited or rural places.

All things considered, Funchal is a tourist-friendly location where you can easily get around in English and make transactions using the euro.

ARRIVING IN FUNCHAL

Funchal Airport and Transportation

The main entry point to Funchal and the island of Madeira is Funchal Airport (Aeroporto da Madeira), commonly referred to as Cristiano Ronaldo Madeira International Airport (Aeroporto Internacional da Madeira Cristiano Ronaldo).

Here are some details regarding Funchal's airport and transit choices:

1. **Airport de Funchal (FNC):**

- The airport is conveniently accessible to both the capital and other areas of Madeira, being situated around 15 kilometres (9 miles) east of the city centre of Funchal.

2. **From the airport at Funchal, transportation:**

- **Taxi**: At the airport, taxis are easily accessible. If you would prefer a direct transfer to your lodging, this is a practical choice. It takes 20 to 30 minutes to go to Funchal's city centre.

- **Shuttle Services:** A few resorts and hotels provide their visitors with shuttle services. Find out if your lodging offers this service by contacting them.

- **Public Bus:** SAM (Sociedade de Automóveis da Madeira) runs a public bus service that links the airport to Funchal and other areas of the island.

    You can check SAM's website or the airport for bus schedules and routes.

- **Car Rental:** You can rent a car to tour the island at your speed from firms who have counters at the Funchal Airport. If necessary, make sure you have an international driver's licence.

- **Private Transfers**: Several suppliers allow you to schedule private transfers in advance to your lodging. Convenience and individualised service are provided by this choice.

3. **Travelling Around Funchal:**

- Many of Funchal's attractions may be reached on foot if you stay in or close to the city centre. The city is walkable.

- Horários do Funchal's public buses offer an affordable means of getting about the city and to other parts of Madeira.

- Taxis are widely accessible and can be called via phone apps or by hailing one on the street.

- Unique transportation options in the city include the native "toboggan" rides, funiculars, and cable cars.

4. How to Navigate Madeira

- Renting a car will enable you to travel to places like the breathtaking Levada treks and the picturesque coastal locations if you intend to explore more of the island.

- Funchal is connected to other towns and areas of Madeira by bus services. Look up the schedules for the routes that work best for your itinerary.

- For day outings or excursions to other areas of the island, taxis, and private transfers can also be scheduled.

Accessing Funchal and touring the stunning island of Madeira during your vacation is very simple thanks to the airport and the accessible transportation choices.

Regardless of your travel plans—whether you're staying in Funchal or going elsewhere—you can discover adequate transportation options.

Navigating the City

Funchal is a pleasant place to explore because it is small, walkable, and has good access to a range of transit alternatives.

To help you get around Funchal and make the most of your trip, here is a guide:

1. **Strolling**:

   - It's preferable to explore Funchal's city centre on foot. You may explore its cobblestone streets, unearth hidden treasures, and enjoy the scenic vistas.

   - With its narrow cobblestone lanes, vibrant architecture, and an abundance of stores, cafes, and restaurants, Zona Velha, also known as Old Town, is a pedestrian-friendly neighbourhood.

2. **Using public transit**

   - Horários do Funchal runs a dependable public bus system in Funchal. The city's numerous neighbourhoods and attractions are connected by buses. Visit bus stops or check the schedule and routes online.

3. **Funiculars and Cable Cars:**
   - Funchal offers unique transportation options, including picturesque trips on cable trains and funiculars. The city and bay are breathtakingly visible from the Funchal-Monte cable car.

   Other well-liked options are the Lavradores Market Funicular and the Monte Cable Car.

4. **Taxicabs**
   - In Funchal, taxis are easily found and can be hailed on the street or from specially designated taxi stands. Taxis are an easy way to get throughout the city and to certain locations.

5. **Rental Cars:**
   - Renting a car is not essential for getting around the city core, but it can be helpful if you want to see more of the island of Madeira. Numerous

car-rental companies have offices in the city and at the Funchal Airport.

6. **Navigational apps and maps:**

- Use a smartphone navigation software or carry a map of Funchal to help you find your way around the city. Popular apps like Google Maps may be trusted to help you find points of interest.

7. **Regional Expertise:**

- Never be afraid to ask locals for advice or directions. Madeirans are renowned for being amiable and frequently delighted to help visitors.

8. **Tour Guides:**

- Participating in guided walking tours or excursions can be an excellent way to discover the city while gaining knowledge about its history, customs, and perspectives from the locals.

9. **Pay Attention to Hills:**

- The city of Funchal lies at different heights, and some of its streets can be quite steep.

  If you have mobility issues, plan your travels carefully and think about taking the funicular or cable cars for trips uphill.

10. **Take a Look Around the Front:**

- The waterfront district of Funchal along Avenida do Mar features a lovely promenade with gardens, sculptures, and views of the ocean. It is a wonderful location for a leisurely walk.

Funchal's modest size and quaint ambiance make it easy to navigate, letting you take your time taking in the city's distinctive fusion of history, culture, and natural beauty.

Funchal is an easy city to visit and enjoy, whether you choose to walk around on foot, take public transportation, or make use of taxis and cable cars.

EXPLORING THE CITY

The Heart of Funchal

The historic city centre of Funchal is the centre of the city, offering a vivid fusion of local life, history, and culture. Here's a deeper look at the main landmarks and attractions that form Funchal's core:

1. **The Funchal Cathedral, or Sé Catedral de Funchal:**
   - The centrepiece of the city is this magnificent, fifteenth-century cathedral. The Gothic and Moorish architectural features bear witness to the rich heritage of Funchal.

2. **The Municipal Square, or Praça do Município:**
   - A quaint square encircled by restaurants, cafes, and old buildings.

It's a nice spot to have lunch or coffee while soaking up the local vibes.

3. **Funchal Market (Mercado dos Lavradores):**

- a vibrant, busy market with fresh fruit, exotic flowers, and handmade items from the Madeerea region.

  For those who enjoy food and culture, it's a sensory experience that shouldn't be missed.

4. **Arriaga Avenue:**

- This graceful boulevard is Funchal's main thoroughfare. It provides a lovely stroll with shops, cafes, and views of the sea along its tree-lined perimeter.

5. **The Municipal Garden, or Jardim Municipal:**

- a lovely park with a duck pond, unique vegetation, and fountains. In the middle of the city, it offers a tranquil haven.

6. **Marina Funchal:**

- The marina offers a lovely setting with colourful boats, waterfront eateries, and views of the Atlantic Ocean. It is the starting point for a variety of water activities.

7. **Santa Maria Street:**

- This attractive and ancient street in Funchal is well-known for its vibrant doors and unusual art project, in which local artists have painted the doors all along the street.

8. **Fort James, or Forte de São Tiago:**

- A 17th-century fort with a café and museum facing the sea. It is a fragment of the marine past of Funchal.

9. **Baltazar Dias Municipal Theater, often known as Theatro Municipal:**

    - a sophisticated theatre renowned for its cultural events and neoclassical architecture.

10. **Festivals and Cultural Events**: -

    - Throughout the year, festivals and other cultural events frequently revolve around the heart of Funchal.

    Don't pass up the chance to attend street festivals, art shows, and local music events.

11. **Local Cuisine**:

- There are a ton of eateries and cafes in the city centre that provide authentic Madeiran fare, such as "espetada" and "black scabbardfish." Savour the flavours of the region and experience Madeira.

Discovering the core of Funchal entails travelling through centuries of history and culture, allowing you to experience the very best of Madeira.

Travellers find this region to be appealing because it embodies the character and soul of the city, from its colourful markets, lush gardens, and local flavours to its historic architecture.

Historical and Cultural Sites

When you visit Funchal, you can experience a wide range of historical and cultural monuments. The city is rich in both history and culture. The following are some of the must-see locations that provide an insight into Funchal and Madeira's history:

1. **The Funchal Cathedral, or Sé Catedral de Funchal:**

    - One of Funchal's oldest buildings is this cathedral, which dates to the fifteenth century. Its architecture is a fusion of styles, with Moorish and Gothic elements.

2. **The Museum of Sacred Art, or Museu de Arte Sacra:**

    - This museum, which is housed in a former bishop's palace, features an amazing collection of religious artwork and relics, such as paintings and sculptures.

3. **Quinta das Cruzes Museum:**
   - Housed in a mediaeval mansion, the museum offers insight into Madeira's history and culture through its varied collection of artwork, furniture, and decorative items.

4. **The Cristiano Ronaldo Museum, or Museu CR7:**
   - This museum, which honours the life and career of the renowned football player Cristiano Ronaldo, who is from Madeira, is a must-visit for football enthusiasts.

5. **The Fort of Saint James, or Forte de São Tiago:**
   - This 17th-century fort gives sweeping views of the city and the sea, as well as an insight into Funchal's maritime past.

The Museum of Contemporary Art is housed there.

6. **Museum of Embroidery and Madeiran Boat, or Museu do Bordado e do Barco Madeirense:**
    - Traditional needlework and boat building are two significant facets of Madeiran culture that are honoured in this museum.

7. **Our Lady of the Mount Church, Igreja de Nossa Senhora do Monte:**
    - This chapel, which is situated in the charming village of Monte, is well-known for both its lovely surroundings and the Monte Toboggan Rides history.

8. **Igreja do Colégio or Church of College:**
    - This church is a magnificent example of Baroque architecture, with

elaborately carved altars and an elaborate interior.

9. **Baltazar Dias Municipal Theater, often known as Theatro Municipal:**

- a sophisticated neoclassical theatre that presents musical, dance, and drama events.

10. **Old Town, or Zona Velha:** -

- Zona Velha, Funchal's historic centre, is a labyrinth of winding cobblestone lanes dotted with brightly coloured buildings, eateries, cafes, and retail establishments. By itself, it's a cultural centre.

11. **Rua de Santa Maria:**

- This quaint street in Funchal is well-known for its "Art of Open Doors" initiative, in which local artists have painted doors to create an outdoor exhibition of art.

You'll have a greater grasp of Funchal's history and its place in Madeira's larger cultural mosaic by visiting these historical and cultural locations.

Every location provides a distinctive viewpoint on the history and creative expression of the island, ensuring an enlightening and rewarding stay.

Local Cuisine and Dining

A fascinating gastronomic scene showcasing the tastes and customs of Madeiran cuisine can be found in Funchal. Enjoy the following regional cuisine and dining establishments while visiting Funchal:

1. **Espetada**

    - A traditional Madeiran dish made of marinated and grilled beef skewers, usually seasoned with bay leaves, salt, and garlic. It's frequently served with traditional Madeiran bread or fried corn.

2. **Espada, or Black Scabbardfish:**

    - Seafood lovers should not miss this fish, a local specialty that is usually served with a sauce made from passion fruit or bananas.

3. **Caco Bolo:**

    - a warm, round, mildly sweet bread that's frequently served with garlic butter. It's a well-liked side dish and snack.

4. **Grelhadas Lapas:**

- Grilled limpets, a kind of marine snail, are a popular specialty in the area. Garlic sauce is usually offered with them.

5. **Gazpacho (Tomato Soup):**

- a thick tomato soup that is loaded with veggies and frequently has a poached egg on top.

6. **Madeirense Bacalhau:**

- A codfish meal made in the Madeiran style, typically made with potatoes, onions, garlic, and olive oil.

7. **Frito Milho:**

- Crispy on the exterior and tender inside, deep-fried maize is a favourite snack or side dish.

8. Poncha:

- Poncha, the traditional alcoholic drink of Madeira, is a cocktail composed of honey, citrus juice (often lemon), and aguardiente, a local sugar cane liquor. It's a strong, refreshing beverage.

9. regional wine

- Madeira is well-known for its eponymous fortified wine. Make sure to try this delightful and unusual wine. You can also go sampling at nearby wineries.

10. Customary Desserts from Madagascar:

- Savor classic desserts like "Pastéis de Nata" (custard tarts), "Queijadas" (cheese tarts), and "Bolo de Mel" (honey cake).

11. **Eating Experiences: -**

    - Savour regional cuisine while taking in views of the ocean at one of Funchal's charming restaurants, particularly those in the Zona Velha. Traditional Madeiran cuisine and fresh fish are served in several places.

12. **Farmers' Markets:**

    - Check out the fresh produce, spices, and traditional Madeiran cuisine items at the Mercado dos Lavradores in Funchal. Sample some local cheeses and unique fruits.

13. **Street Food and Snacks: -**

    - While exploring the city, don't pass up the chance to sample street food and snacks like "bifana" (pork sandwich) and "tremoços" (salted lupini beans).

14. **Al Fresco Dining:**

- A lot of Funchal restaurants have outdoor seating, so you may eat outside while taking in views of the city and the sea.

South American, Portuguese, and African culinary traditions have all affected the delicious flavour blend that is Madeiran food. Discovering the regional food and dining in Funchal is a sensory experience that is a must-do when visiting Madeira.

OUTDOOR ADVENTURES

This is a comprehensive guide to Funchal, Madeira's outdoor activities, which include parks and botanical gardens, hiking and nature trails, and water sports and activities:

Outdoor Activities in Madeira's Funchal

Trekking and Natural Pathways:

For those who love the great outdoors, Funchal and its environs are a heaven. A wide variety of hiking and nature routes may be found in Madeira thanks to its untamed terrain and lush surroundings. What you should know is as follows:

1. **Levada Walks:** The island of Madeira is well-known for its Levadas, which are winding irrigation ditches. A system of trekking paths is made possible by these Levadas, which wind through

forests, beside waterfalls, and along cliff faces. Levada das 25 Fontes, Levada do Caniçal, and Levada do Caldeirão Verde are a few famous Levada walks. *or Levada das Tornos*

2. **Pico do Arieiro**: The third-highest peak on the island, Pico do Arieiro, is a walk worth taking if you're looking for something more strenuous. The trail provides amazing sweeping views of the interior of the island.

   Bus 2   No 8

3. Discover the historic Laurissilva Forest, recognized as a UNESCO World Heritage Site and renowned for its ancient laurel trees and distinctive flora. This lovely woodland has a lot of well-marked routes.

4. Visits with indigenous species and breathtaking treks through laurel forests may be found in Santana and

Ribeiro Frio. Not far from Ribeiro Frio, the Balcoes Viewpoint provides breathtaking views.

Water Sports & Recreation:

1. **Snorkelling and diving**: Madeira's crystal-clear seas are perfect for these activities. Discover vibrant marine life, shipwrecks, and underwater caverns.

2. **Surfing**: The northern coast of the island is a favourite destination for surfers due to its great waves.

3. Take a boat excursion from Funchal's marina to see whales, dolphins, and other marine animals in their native environment.

4. **Kayaking and canoeing**: Explore the island's numerous rivers and lakes or paddle beside the coast. Kayaking on

the Bay of Funchal is a great experience.

5. **Canyoning**: If you're looking for a thrilling experience, consider canyoning in the harsh and steep valleys of Madeira. It combines swimming, climbing, and rappelling.

Parks and Botanical Gardens:

1. Beautiful parks and gardens in Funchal allow you to fully appreciate Madeira's natural splendour.

2. **Monte Palace Tropical Garden**: With its elaborate tile panels, koi ponds, and exotic species from all over the world, this botanical garden is a real gem. There is a museum in the park that displays the history of Madeira.

3. The Madeira Botanical Garden, or Jardim Botânico da Madeira, offers a wide variety of native, exotic, and endemic plants for display.

   Magnificent views of Funchal and the Atlantic Ocean may be seen from the garden.

4. **Parque de Santa Catarina:** With its vibrant flower beds, fountains, and statues, this urban park is ideal for a stroll. It's the perfect location for a relaxed afternoon or picnic.

5. **Palheiro Gardens:** These lush, tranquil gardens are just a short drive from Funchal. A wide range of plants are present, such as azaleas and camellias.

Discovering the tranquil parks and botanical gardens, as well as the exhilarating water sports and hiking along Levadas, offers a comprehensive understanding of Funchal's natural beauty and outdoor recreational options. Funchal has something for any nature lover, whether they are looking for action or peace.

HIDDEN GEMS AND LOCAL SECRETS

Off the Beaten Path Attractions

Discovering off-the-beaten-path sites in Funchal, Madeira, lets you get a fresh perspective on the city and its surrounds and unearth hidden jewels. Here are a few lesser-known locations and things to do while you're there:

1. The Real Caminho da Madeira

- This ancient royal path provides a less-explored option to the well-known Levada hikes.

  It offers a more sedate hiking experience by passing through quaint villages, woodlands, and isolated areas.

2. **The Neve Poço:**

- Poço da Neve is an interesting historical site that dates back to the 18th century. It was an old ice plant where ice was delivered and kept for use in the city.

  The guided tour provides information about the history of ice manufacture in Madeira.

3. **Seixal and Ribeira Funda:**

- From Funchal, go northwest to the sleepy settlement of Seixal and the nearby Ribeira Funda.

  Discover the natural ponds and beaches with black sand here, and take in the quieter side of the shore.

4. **Fanal Vereda:**

- Hiking through a mysterious forest of old laurel trees, this track is comparatively unexplored. Steps away from the busier trails, this stroll is serene and enchanted.

5. **Centre for Volcanism and São Vicente Caves:**

- São Vicente's volcanic caves and the Volcanism Center offer unique insights into the island's geological history, even though they're not completely off the main path.

6. **Ponta de São Lourenço and Caniçal:**

- Discover the unusual vegetation and dry landscapes of Ponta de São Lourenço, located near the eastern extremity of the island. The surrounding fishing village of Caniçal provides an insight into local life.

7. The Father's Day:

- This remote winery and farm, only reachable by boat or cable car, has a tranquil ambiance. You can unwind while taking in the stunning views of the seaside or have dinner at the restaurant.

8. Ferreiro Palheiro:

- This quaint village is well-known for its breathtaking surroundings and quaint houses. It's a great location for a stroll and a getaway from the bustle.

9. Madeira Natural Park, o Parque Natural da Madeira:

- For lovers of the outdoors, the entire island is a treasure trove. Discover more secluded parts of the Madeira Natural Park to see pristine scenery, rare species of flora, and unusual fauna.

10. **Gardens at Monte Palace: -**

- This garden, which is frequently eclipsed by the Monte Palace Tropical Garden, has lovely views, a variety of modern sculptures, and a calm environment.

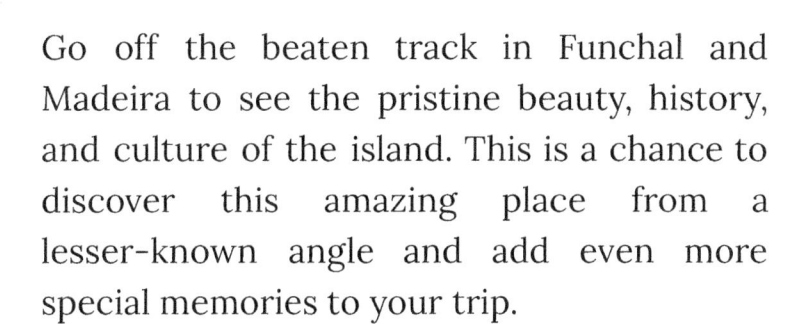

Go off the beaten track in Funchal and Madeira to see the pristine beauty, history, and culture of the island. This is a chance to discover this amazing place from a lesser-known angle and add even more special memories to your trip.

Funchal's Best-Kept Secrets

Uncovering the most well-kept secrets of Funchal might enhance your vacation with a dash of mystery and surprise. In Funchal, Madeira, there are a few undiscovered treasures and lesser-known attractions.

1. **Forte de São José:** Often disregarded by visitors, this 18th-century fortification is also referred to as the Pico fortification.

   It offers tranquil surroundings and sweeping views of the bay.

2. **Farmers' and Flea Markets:** Funchal features smaller local markets like Mercado da Penteada and Mercado do Livramento, where you may meet locals and find fresh vegetables, handmade goods, and antiques. The Mercado dos Lavradores is a well-known market.

3. **Monte Palace Art Garden:** This undiscovered treasure, which is close to the Monte Palace Tropical Garden, offers peaceful exhibitions of modern art. A peaceful getaway from the city, it is.

4. **Quinta Vigia:** The President of the Regional Government of Madeira resides in this old mansion with a lovely garden. The public can enjoy the breathtaking views of Funchal from the grounds, even though you are unable to tour the interior.

5. **Praia Formosa Beach Caves:** This unique, undiscovered area along the shore is revealed by the caverns and tunnels chiselled into the rocks at Praia Formosa Beach.

6. **Rua de Santa Maria Street Art**: There are sculptures, murals, and a lively

environment in this artistic and colourful Zona Velha neighbourhood. For those who stray beyond the beaten roads, it is a joyful surprise and a priceless find for art enthusiasts.

7. **Trilho das 25 Fontes**: The breathtaking "25 Fontes" (25 Springs) waterfall is reached by this lesser-known Levada trail. Compared to other of the busier Levada treks, it's less busy.

8. Igreja de Nossa Senhora do Bom Sucesso: This little church, which is tucked away in the Zona Velha neighbourhood of Funchal, is a hidden gem with an elaborate interior that many visitors overlook.

9. **Zona Velha Rooftop Bars**: Discover quaint rooftop bars with views of the city and the Atlantic by meandering through the neighbourhood's tiny

lanes. These are great for relaxing since they are frequently quiet.

10. **Mercado do Abasto de Funchal:** A little-known neighbourhood market where you can get a taste of local culture, buy fresh produce, and eat basic, regional cuisine from stand-alone vendors.

11. **Secret Courtyards:** The old town of Funchal is full of quaint squares and secret courtyards. Spend some time exploring these peaceful areas of the city.

These best-kept secrets and hidden jewels in Funchal provide visitors with an alternative viewpoint on the city and provide unforgettable experiences that go beyond the standard tourist traps.

Your trip to Funchal can be made even more memorable by visiting these lesser-known locations.

Meeting the Locals

Among the most enriching experiences you may have while visiting Funchal, Madeira, is getting to know and interact with the locals. The following advice can help you establish a rapport with the amiable and hospitable locals:

1. **Acquire Some Basic Portuguese words:** Even though the majority of people in Funchal understand English.

    It can be helpful to show respect for the local way of life and break the ice by learning a few basic Portuguese words. It is appreciated when people use expressions like "Olá" (hello), "Obrigado/a" (thank you), and "Por favour" (please).

2. **Regular Local Establishments:** Visit markets, cafes, and restaurants in your community. These are excellent locations to mingle, make suggestions, and engage in discussion with the locals. You'll see more familiar people the more times you visit.

3. **Take Part in Local Festivals and Events:** Look for festivals, concerts, and cultural events on the local event calendar. These events offer fantastic chances to interact with people and take in their customs and festivals.

4. **Take Part in Guided Tours and Workshops**: Getting to know locals who are enthusiastic about sharing their knowledge can be entertaining

and enlightening when you take part in cooking lessons, guided tours, or workshops.

5. **Volunteer or Take Part in Community Activities:** Seek for chances to volunteer or engage in community events that will enable you to support your neighbourhood while making new friends who have similar interests and values.

6. **Go to a Fado Performance:** Fado is the traditional music of Portugal. You may meet other music lovers and get a taste of the Portuguese way of life by going to a Fado performance.

7. **Investigate the communities:** Go beyond the popular tourist destinations and investigate the many Funchal communities. Every area has

its distinct personality, and its people take great pride in their local history.

8. **Choose Local Accommodations**: Take into consideration booking a room in a guesthouse, bed & breakfast, or a locally owned vacation rental. These lodgings frequently provide a more intimate and immersive experience.

9. **Be Inquisitive and Open:** Enter into conversations with an open mind and a curious demeanour. Engage in active listening, pose questions, and show that you genuinely want to learn about the experiences and tales of the individuals you meet.

10. **Respect Local customs:** Pay attention to the traditions and customs of the area. You will gain the favour of the people and have more meaningful

relationships if you educate yourself about and appreciate the culture.

Making local acquaintances in Funchal can result in enduring relationships, insightful understandings of the way of life there, and a greater appreciation of Madeira's rich cultural heritage.

The friendly and welcoming demeanour of the inhabitants in Funchal facilitates meaningful interactions and the creation of enduring memories throughout your stay.

DAY TRIPS AND EXCURSIONS

✓ Bus tour

Exploring Beyond Funchal

Discovering Madeira's varied and breathtaking scenery is possible by venturing outside of Funchal. When travelling outside of the capital, take into account the following must-see locations and things to do:

1. **São Vicente:** ✓   1 x 7
   - This quaint village on the island's northern shore is well-known for its scenic church, natural caves, and the São Vicente Caves and Volcanism Center, which teaches visitors about the island's volcanic past.

2. **Santana** ✓   2 x 6
   - Santana, which is well-known for its unique "palheiros," or triangle thatched dwellings, offers an insight into

Madeira's rural lifestyle. A visit to the Madeira Theme Park is highly recommended.

3. **Sol's Ponta:**

- One of the sunniest locations on the island is this charming seaside village. Unwind on the beach with black sand while exploring the neighbouring levadas and rocks.

4. **The Brava River:**

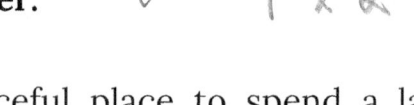

- It's a peaceful place to spend a lazy afternoon—a small seaside town with a lovely church, a sandy beach, and a promenade.

5. **Calahaite**

- Calheta, well-known for its artificial golden sand beach, is a terrific spot to unwind and experience water activities like kayaking and stand-up paddleboarding.

6. **Lobos Camara:** ✓ 1 × 8

- A charming fishing town that Winston Churchill had a fondness for painting. It's a terrific place to take in the fishing culture of the area.

7. **Nun's Valley, or Curral das Freiras:**

- This isolated valley, tucked away in the mountains, was originally a nunnery retreat and offers breathtaking vistas and hiking options.

8. **Moniz de Porto:** ✓ 1½ hrs B 1 × 5

- Porto Moniz, well-known for its organic rock pools, is a special place to swim and unwind in a natural environment.

9. Frio Ribeiro:

- Notable for its trout farm and proximity to other Levada hikes, including the Levada dos Balcoes, it is a serene location within the forest.

10. São Lourenço Ponta: -

- The island's easternmost point offers striking views and an arid, dramatic terrain with unusual rock formations. This is an amazing place to hike.

11. The Laurissilva Forest:

- With its prehistoric laurel trees, distinctive flora, and peaceful hiking trails, discover the historic Laurissilva Forest, a UNESCO World Heritage Site.

12. **The Western shore of Madeira:**

- Take in the untamed splendour of Madeira's western shore, which is home to towering cliffs and breathtaking views.

  In this region, the village of Paul do Mar is a hidden treasure.

13. **Pico Ruivo:**

- Climb to the island's highest summit, Pico Ruivo, for expansive vistas of the heart of Madeira.

14. **North Coast Beaches: -**

- Find secluded beaches that offer a tranquil getaway on the north coast, such as Prainha.

You may explore Madeira's varied landscapes, quaint communities, and exceptional natural wonders by travelling outside of Funchal.

There are many ways to make your trip to Madeira unforgettable, whether your interests are hiking, discovering the island's culture, or just taking in the breathtaking scenery.

Island Hopping Adventures

Even while Madeira is a fantastic vacation in and of itself, the archipelago provides island-hopping experiences to discover neighbouring islands, each with a distinct charm.

Consider visiting these nearby islands for your island-hopping excursions from Madeira:

1. **Santo Porto:**

    - Porto Santo, which is 40 kilometres northeast of Madeira, is renowned for its peaceful waters and golden sand beaches.

        From Funchal, you may travel by ferry to Porto Santo, where you can discover the tranquil island's breathtaking scenery.

2. **Islands of the Desert (Ilhas Desertas):**

    - This little archipelago is located southeast of Madeira. The Desertas Islands are a nature reserve containing distinctive plants and animals, such as monk seals, and are deserted.

        You can go on nature exploration or day trips with boat tours.

3. **Ilhas Selvagens, or the Savage Islands:**

   - The Savage Islands, located further south of Madeira, are likewise a designated nature reserve.

     Their biodiversity and immaculate scenery are well-known. Those who enjoy nature and birdwatching can take day trips to the Selvagens.

4. **Islands of Canary:**

   - The Canary Islands, which include Tenerife and Gran Canaria, are not a part of the Madeira archipelago, although they are reasonably close and may be reached from Funchal by ferry or quick plane.

     These islands provide a variety of activities, lively cultures, and varied landscapes.

5. **The Azores**

- Despite being far away from Madeira, the Azores archipelago provides exceptional chances for island hopping.

    These volcanic islands, renowned for their beautiful landscapes, geothermal spas, and outdoor experiences, are reachable by plane from Madeira.

Think about your hobbies, the amount of time you have available, and your preferred means of transportation when organising an island-hopping trip from Madeira.

Island hopping allows you to take in a wider range of Atlantic beauty and culture, whether you decide to visit the neighbouring Porto Santo, discover the unspoiled wilderness of the Desertas and Selvagens, or travel to the Canary Islands or Azores.

Tips for Organizing Day Trips

Planning day trips from Madeira's Funchal can be a fun way to discover the island and its environs. The following advice can help you organise and maximise your day trips:

1. **Make a plan beforehand:**

    - Make a rough schedule of the places and activities you wish to see and experience. Think about the separations and durations of travel between the destinations.

2. **Select Your Mode of Transit:**

    - Choose if you want to hire a private driver, rent a car, take a guided trip, or utilise public transit.

    Your decision will be influenced by your tastes, financial situation, and how easily you can go to the places you've selected.

3. **Verify the Opening Hours:**

- Check the hours of operation for the restaurants, attractions, and any particular locations you intend to visit. Certain locations might have restricted hours or be closed on specific days.

4. **Bring Necessities:**

- Make sure you have all the necessities, like a map or GPS device, a reusable water bottle, suitable shoes, sunscreen, and any necessary tickets or identification.

5. **Pay Attention to the Weather:**

- Examine the day's weather prediction and make appropriate packing decisions. Given how unpredictable Madeira's weather may be, it's a smart idea to pack for a variety of scenarios.

6. **Meals and Snacks:**

- If you intend to visit somewhere with few dining alternatives, bring snacks or a picnic lunch. When you get there, think about sampling the local food.

7. **Honour the environment and local laws:**

- To preserve the environment, abide by the Leave No Trace philosophy when exploring natural regions. Recognize the laws and customs of the area.

8. **Remain Up to Date:**

- Make sure you have access to current information to aid in your navigation and discovery of sites of interest, such as a local map, guidebook, or navigation app.

9. Safety comes first:

- Tell someone about your intended day trip, and in case of emergency, carry a fully charged phone or other method of communication. Be cautious at all times when venturing into new areas.

10. Savour Your Flexibility:

- Stay receptive to unexpected turns and discoveries as you go. When you deviate off the path, you may have some of the most amazing experiences.

11. Capture Memories: -

- Don't forget your smartphone or camera to take pictures of the lovely surroundings and special moments throughout your day trip.

12. **Encourage Local Businesses:**

- To help the community's economy, try to make purchases of products and services from nearby companies.

13. Look for Special Events: -

- In the location you intend to visit, keep an eye out for any festivals, special events, or local happenings. Your day trip experience can be improved by going to local activities.

14. **Make a Timely Return: -**

- If you're visiting more isolated or wild regions, make sure you schedule your day so you have enough time to get back to Funchal before dusk.

With these pointers, you may make the most of your time and have an unforgettable and pleasurable day trip from Funchal, admiring Madeira's stunning scenery and distinctive culture.

PRACTICAL INFORMATION

Accommodation Options

A variety of lodging choices are available in Funchal, Madeira, to accommodate a range of tastes and price ranges. When making your plans to Funchal, keep the following lodging options in mind:

1. **Hotels**: There are many different types of hotels in Funchal, ranging from boutique and affordable lodgings to opulent five-star resorts. A lot of hotels provide restaurants, spas, pools, and breathtaking views of the ocean as facilities.

2. **Guesthouses and Bed and Breakfasts**: These lodging options are great if you'd like a more private and tailored experience. As part of your stay, they

frequently provide breakfast and quaint lodging.

3. **Vacation Rentals**: If you want a more homey experience, you can rent condos, flats, or villas. Longer stays and those who wish to have the freedom to prepare their meals can benefit greatly from vacation rentals.

4. **Hostels**: A few hostels in Funchal are ideal for backpackers and those on a tight budget. Hostels provide both private and dorm-style accommodations, fostering a social setting for meeting other visitors.

5. **Apart-hotels:** These blend the flexibility of an apartment with the ease of a hotel. They frequently have separate living areas and kitchens.

6. **Resorts**: Madeira is well-known for its opulent resorts, some of which are situated in tranquil, picturesque settings outside of Funchal. High-end facilities and services are provided by these resorts.

7. **Rural tourist Accommodations**: If you're looking for a distinctive experience, think about booking a stay at a rural tourist establishment, which is frequently found in Madeira's stunning countryside. Cottages and country homes are examples of this.

8. **Eco-Friendly lodging**: Madeira is renowned for its unspoiled beauty, and you may stay in balance with the environment by staying in eco-friendly lodging.

9. **Pousadas**: These are distinctive or historic lodgings that provide a sense

of culture and tradition. They are frequently housed in heritage structures.

10. **Budget and Chain Hotels:** Funchal has a selection of reasonably priced chain hotels to suit the needs of tourists on a tight budget, guaranteeing a comfortable stay without going over budget.

11. **Luxurious Villas:** If you're looking for an incredibly lavish vacation, think about renting a luxury villa with features like private pools and breathtaking views.

Think about your interests, financial constraints, and the kind of experience you're looking for when selecting a place to stay in Funchal. To guarantee your chosen accommodation, it's also a good idea to reserve in advance, particularly during the busiest travel seasons. It's possible to locate hotels in Funchal that will improve your Madeira trip, regardless of your preferences for adventure, relaxation, or a combination of the two.

Health and Safety Tips

It is crucial to make sure you are safe and healthy when visiting Funchal, Madeira. When exploring the city and the island, bear the following health and safety advice in mind:

Safety Advice:

1. Consider acquiring travel insurance that provides coverage for unanticipated circumstances such as

medical emergencies and trip cancellations.

2. **Emergency Numbers**: Be aware of the local emergency numbers in Madeira, which are 291 700 112 for local emergency services, and 112 for general emergencies.

3. **Weather Awareness**: Pay attention to the weather, particularly if you have any outside plans. Because of Madeira's unpredictable weather, dress appropriately.

4. **Sun Protection**: The sun may be very intense in Madeira. To avoid being sunburned, use sunscreen, cover yourself with a hat, and shield your skin from UV rays.

5. Drink lots of water to stay hydrated, especially on warm days when you're

sightseeing or doing physical activities. Stay hydrated since dehydration can be dangerous.

6. **Safety on Levada Walks:** Exercise caution when approaching the edges and heed safety instructions if you intend to trek the Levadas. Certain routes may be confined and vulnerable.

7. **Swimming Safety:** Exercise caution when swimming in the sea, particularly on unguarded beaches. Observe currents and adhere to regional safety regulations.

8. **Crime Awareness:** Although Funchal is a relatively safe place to visit, take the standard safety precautions. In crowded places, watch out for your possessions and use caution around pickpockets.

9. **Local Traditions:** Honour regional traditions and customs. Since churches and other places of worship are important parts of Funchal's Catholic heritage, it is advisable to dress modestly while visiting them.

Health Advice:

1. **Travel Insurance:** As previously indicated, it's critical to have travel insurance that includes medical emergencies.

2. **Health Preparations:** See your doctor before your travel to make sure you have received all recommended immunizations and to address any concerns you may have.

3. **Medications & Prescriptions:** Bring a copy of your prescriptions with you

and make sure you have enough of your prescribed drugs for the trip.

4. **Medical Facilities:** Learn where the hospitals and pharmacies are located in Funchal in case you require medical attention.

5. **Protection from Insects:** Although there is no chance of malaria in Madeira, it is still a good idea to wear protective gear against insect bites when in forested areas.

6. **Food and Water Safety:** Madeira has excellent food safety standards; but, if you're worried about tap water, exercise caution and drink bottled water.

7. **COVID-19 Precautions:** Keep abreast of the most recent COVID-19 recommendations and limitations, and

heed the guidance of your local health authorities. Mask-wearing and social isolation are two examples of this.

8. **Outdoor Activity Safety**: Make sure you participate in risky activities like canyoning with qualified guides and heed their safety advice.

9. **Allergies & Dietary Restrictions**: When dining out, be sure to let them know if you have any dietary requirements or food allergies.

While it's true that Funchal's emergency services are prepared to manage a wide range of circumstances, being proactive is the key to a secure and pleasurable trip. Stay safe and healthy throughout your journey to Funchal and the stunning island of Madeira.

Useful Phrases and Etiquette

You can improve your trip to Funchal, Madeira, by learning a few basic phrases in Portuguese and being aware of local manners. The following are some helpful expressions and manners to remember:

Practical Phrases in Portuguese:

- Hello: "Olá" (oh-LAH)
- Good morning: "Bom dia" (bohm DEE-ah)
- Good afternoon: "Boa tarde" (boh-ah TAHR-deh)
- Good evening/night: "Boa noite" (boh-ah NOH-ee-teh)
- Please: "Por favor" (por fah-VOHR)
- Thank you: "Obrigado" (oh-bree-GAH-doh) for males, "Obrigada" (oh-bree-GAH-dah) for females
- You're welcome: "De nada" (dee NAH-dah)

- Yes: "Sim" (seem)
- No: "Não" (nah-oh)
- Excuse me/pardon: "Com licença" (kohm lee-SEN-sah)
- I'm sorry: "Desculpe" (deh-SKOOL-peh)
- Do you speak English? "Fala inglês?" (FAH-lah een-GLAYSH?)
- How much does this cost? "Quanto custa isto?" (KWAN-toh KOOS-tah EES-too?)
- Where is...? "Onde fica...?" (OHN-dee FEE-kah...?)
- I don't understand: "Não entendo" (NAH-oh ehn-TEN-doh)

Etiquette advice

1. **Politeness**: In Portuguese society, being courteous is highly regarded. Make regular use of "obrigado" (thank you) and "por favor" (please).

2. **Salutation**: Depending on the time of day, extend a cordial "Bom dia" (good morning), "boa tarde" (good afternoon), or "boa noite" (good evening/night) to others.

3. **Tipping**: It is traditional to leave a gratuity in restaurants, typically between 10% and 15% of the total cost.

4. **Dress Modestly**: Cover your knees and shoulders when you enter places of worship like churches. It is customary to take off your sunglasses and hat when you enter a place of worship.

5. **Use Cutlery:** Even with finger foods, when dining, use cutlery to eat rather than your hands.

6. Respectfully wait your turn in lines or queues while exercising patience.

Shoving and pushing are regarded as rude behaviors.

7. **Punctuality**: Be on time for meetings and appointments. It's often considered rude to be late.

8. **Public Conduct:** Steer clear of boisterous and obnoxious behaviour in public areas. Be polite and composed at all times.

9. **Kissing to welcome**: Friends and acquaintances typically kiss each other on both cheeks when they welcome each other. It is more customary to shake hands in formal or business contexts.

10. **Language**: Although English is widely spoken in Funchal, it is respectful of the local way of life to attempt to speak a few Portuguese words.

Not only will you be well-received by the locals but also have a more immersive and polite experience during your stay in Funchal, Madeira, if you adhere to these etiquette recommendations and use a few common Portuguese phrases.

FUNCHAL IN 2024: EVENTS AND FESTIVALS

Noteworthy Events and Festivals

All year long, Funchal and Madeira are home to several notable celebrations and events. This is a great chance to fully immerse oneself in the customs and culture of the area during these festivals. The following are a few of Funchal's most prominent celebrations and events:

1. The Madeira Carnival (Carnaval da Madeira) is one of Portugal's biggest and most colourful celebrations.

   Parades, vibrant costumes, street dancing, and music are all part of it. The centrepiece is the Funchal Carnival Parade, which features intricate floats and samba dancers.

2. **Madeira Flower Festival (Festa da Flor):** This springtime event honours the vibrant blooms that adorn the island.

   The centrepiece event is the Flower Parade, which takes place across Funchal and features elaborately decorated flowery floats and participants dressed in flower-themed costumes.

3. The Atlantic Festival, also known as the Festival do Atlântico, is a June celebration that includes several fireworks shows, musical performances, and entertainment by the Funchal waterfront.

   The International Fireworks Competition is the main event, where pyrotechnic displays from various nations are competed.

4. The Madeira Wine Festival, also known as the Festa do Vinho, is an August celebration of the island's wine culture. Traditional folklore performances, wine tastings, and grape stomping are among the events.

5. Madeira New Year's Eve (Fim de Ano no Funchal): One of the biggest and most impressive fireworks shows in the world takes place in Funchal on New Year's Eve. To celebrate the new year, the entire city comes to life with music, lights, and celebrations.

6. The September Columbus Festival, also known as the Festa de Colombo, pays tribute to Christopher Columbus, who may have resided on Madeira before he explored the Americas. A recreation of his arrival is one of the festival's many historical and cultural events.

7. **Madeira Wine Rally (Rali Vinho da Madeira):** Usually held in August, this rally is a significant motorsport event. It draws competitors from all over the world who take on the island's winding and difficult roads.

8. **Festivities for Christmas and New Year's:** Madeira is renowned for its charming decorations for these holidays. Millions of lights cover the entire city, illuminating it and fostering a wonderful environment.

   A globally recognized event is the yearly fireworks show on New Year's Eve.

9. **Feast of Our Lady of Monte (Festa de Nossa Senhora do Monte):** Held in August, this religious celebration honours Nossa Senhora do Monte, the

island's patron saint. The procession and pilgrimage to the Monte Church are the main events.

The vivid spirit, customs, and culture of Madeira can be experienced singularly and unforgettably through these celebrations and events. For an amazing experience, make sure to verify the dates and schedule your visit during one of these events.

Planning Your Visit Around Special Occasions

Arranging your vacation in Funchal, Madeira, around holidays and celebrations might give your experience something special and unforgettable. The following advice can help you do that:

1. **Verify Festival Dates:** Find out when the festivals or other special events you're interested in attending are happening. Although these events frequently have set dates every year, it's important to make sure they coincide with the dates of your particular trip.

2. **Reserve Accommodations in Advance:** Funchal can see a large influx of guests during festivals and other noteworthy occasions.

    It's advisable to make reservations well in advance to guarantee your ideal lodging, particularly for well-known occasions like New Year's Eve and the Madeira Carnival.

3. **Arrange Your Itinerary:** After you have the festival dates in mind, arrange your schedule accordingly. Make sure your activities fit in with the festival's schedule by taking into account the festival's key events and their locations.

4. **Discover Local Cuisine**: Seize the chance to enjoy regional delicacies and foods related to the celebration. There are food and drink options at many festivals that are specific to the event.

5. **Honor Local Customs:** Become acquainted with the festival's connected customs and traditions. Participating in local customs and showing respect can improve your experience.

6. **Accept the Atmosphere**: Give yourself over to the celebratory ambiance. Embrace the throng, watch parades,

and take in the dancing and music. Engage in conversation with locals and other tourists without fear.

7. **Capture Memories:** Have your camera or smartphone ready to record the moments.

   Photographic opportunities abound due to the vibrant parades, pyrotechnics, and cultural events.

8. **Be There Early:** To guarantee a decent viewing position for well-attended events like the New Year's Eve fireworks, it's best to be there early. Hours before the advance, crowds can form.

9. **Remain Safe:** Take normal safety precautions and pay attention to your possessions in busy areas. Observe any

instructions that the event organisers may present.

10. **Make a Transportation Plan:** Think about how you're going to and from the festival activities.

    During festivals, parking and traffic might be problematic, so walking or public transportation might be your best bet.

11. **Look up COVID-19 Recommendations:** Remember that there may be particular COVID-19 criteria and limits for festivals and other occasions.

    Keep abreast with the most recent information released by the local government.

Whether you're visiting for the vibrant Carnival, the enchanted New Year's Eve festivities, or other special occasions, scheduling your vacation around these events can enhance the excitement and cultural diversity of your trip to Funchal. Savour the celebrations and the distinct ambiance that each occasion offers to this stunning island.

APPENDICES

Sample Itineraries

These are two possible itineraries for your trip to Madeira's Funchal. These tours take you to see different parts of the city and give you a chance to sample its cuisine, culture, and scenic splendour. They can be changed to suit your stay's duration and your interests.

A Sample Three-Day Schedule

Day 1: Salutations from Funchal

Daybreak:
- Land at the airport in Funchal.
- Take a look at your lodging.

Afterwards:

- Admire the stunning views of the ocean while strolling along the Funchal shoreline.
- Explore the local fruit, flowers, and crafts in the Mercado dos Lavradores (Funchal Market).

Nighttime:

- Visit a nearby restaurant for a traditional Madeiran dinner and sample dishes like "scabbard fish" or "espetada," which are skewered pieces of grilled pork.

Day 2: Take a City Tour

Daybreak:

- Go on an independent exploration of the city or join a guided tour. See places like the São Tiago Fortress and the Funchal Cathedral, or Sede

Catedral de Nossa Senhora da Assunção.

Afterwards:

- Visit the Botanical Garden, Jardim Botânico da Madeira, to take in the breathtaking scenery and abundant vegetation.

- Discover the mediaeval village of Monte as well as the Monte Palace Tropical Garden.

Nighttime:

- Enjoy a meal at a neighbourhood eatery and don't forget to sample a "," a classic Madeiran beverage.

Day 3: Levada Walk and Nature

Daybreak:

- For a cool stroll, plan a trip to the Laurissilva Forest, a UNESCO World Heritage Site.

Afterwards:

- Take a walk on Levada. Select a trail according to your tastes and level of fitness. Levada do Caldeirão Verde and Levada das 25 Fontes are excellent choices.

Nighttime:

- After spending the day in the great outdoors, savour dinner at a restaurant with a view of Funchal.

A Sample Seven-Day Schedule

Day 1: Arrival and Orientation

- Once you reach the airport in Funchal, settle into your lodging.

- Take a stroll along the waterfront in Funchal to unwind by the water's edge.

Day 2: Touring Funchal

- Discover the Mercado dos Lavradores, the Sé Cathedral of Nossa Senhora da Assunção, and the Monte Cable Car as you stroll around Funchal 's ancient area.

Day 3: Culture and Botanical Gardens
- Visit the Jardim Botânico da Madeira in the morning, then spend the afternoon in Funchal visiting museums and other cultural attractions.

Day Four: Journey to Porto Santo
- Go by ferry to Porto Santo, discover the beaches with golden sand, and spend a leisurely day there.

Day 5: Walking Levada and Adventure

- Take up an adventurous sport like paragliding, mountain biking, or canyoning.
- Wander through Levada, maybe along Levada das Rabaçal, in the afternoon.

Day 6: Gastronomic Pleasures and Wine

- To sample Madeira wine, stop by a neighbourhood wine cellar in Funchal.

- Savour a classic Madeiran supper while trying out some of the local cuisine at a restaurant.

Day 7: Farewell and Nature Day

- Explore Madeira's natural beauty on your final day. Visit Ponta de São Lourenço if you're looking for picturesque scenery.

- Have a goodbye meal in Funchal and relish the cuisine for a final time.

These exemplary itineraries combine leisure, food, culture, and the outdoors. These can be modified by your preferences and the particular sights or things you choose to do while visiting Funchal, Madeira.

Useful Contacts and Information

To guarantee a hassle-free and pleasurable journey to Funchal, Madeira, it's critical to have access to helpful contacts and information. You may find the following important contacts and information useful while visiting:

Emergency Numbers:

- Emergency Services: Dial 112 in case of any emergency.
- Police (PSP) Local: 291 215 460
- Department of Fire: 291 700 100
- Emergencies in Medicine: 291 700 400

Information for Travelers:

- Tourist Office: The city centre of Funchal is home to the tourist office, which offers details on events, activities, and attractions in the area.

- Address: 16 Avenida Arriaga, Funchal, 9004-519

- Call: (291) 211-900

- **Website**: Go to the Official Website of Madeira Transportation:

- Cristiano Ronaldo Madeira International Airport (FNC) is the

airport that serves Funchal. Go to the ANA Aeroportos de Portugal website for information about the airport.
- **Public Transportation**: The Horários do Funchal website has details on buses and other transportation options in the city.

Medical Services:

1. The primary hospital in Funchal is called Hospital Central do Funchal.

2. Rua João de Deus, 9004-509 Funchal is the address.

3. Call: (291) 705 600

Consulates and Embassies:

1. Get in touch with the embassy or consulate of your nation in Portugal if you require consular help.

The official government website of your nation has the contact details.

Local Money Exchange and Banking:

- The Euro (EUR) is the currency in use in Madeira. In Funchal, banking services are generally accessible, and ATMs can be found all over the city.

Speech:

- Portuguese is the official language of Madeira. Even though English is widely spoken by locals in Funchal, knowing a few simple Portuguese words can be useful.

Zone of Time:

- The time zone of Madeira is Western European Time (WET). It is in line with

Western European Summer Time (WEST) during daylight saving time.

Climate:

- Madeira experiences variable weather due to its subtropical environment. Throughout your visit, keep track of the local weather forecast.

Regional Events

- If you're looking for information about festivals, events, and special occasions taking place during your visit, check out the local event calendars found on websites like Visit Madeira or local newspapers.

You can traverse Funchal more easily, stay safe, and enjoy your time at this stunning location to the fullest if you have access to these contacts and information.

Printed in Great Britain
by Amazon